CONTENTS

Introduction

This is a short book to get you on the path to the truth and the good life. It includes all facts regarding scriptures, miracles and promises.

The purpose of this book is to help you understand the roles of God, Jesus, and the Holy Spirit and how you need to incorporate His greatness in your life. The words in this book are to encourage you and to guide you to pick up the Holy Bible and read it because God's truth is real and very much alive today! Reading the bible should not be a task it should be something you want to do because you will need these words in this life to teach you, guide you, strengthen you and lean on up until the day you die.

God's word will give you life if you allow it to. I know you may be saying, huh, I am already alive and that does not make any sense, but hear this when negative words are spoken to you, ask yourself, how does that make you feel? Discouraged, sad, sometimes you may even feel like giving up on something, or you may feel hopeless or depressed. It is like something was stolen from you! It takes away the good feelings you may have had. When people speak positive words, how do you feel? Encouraged, happy, strong, hopeful, and even joyful. It adds good feelings to you, and it makes you want to keep going on to achieve whatever goal it is that you are trying to reach or whatever you are trying to accomplish!

In this life's journey you need God's word and after all He started with a word (Genesis 1:3). It will teach you the important things that God is looking for in you, like faith. This is big because it starts there and this matters most to God, believing without seeing, believing God is real and He is a spirit. You cannot see

Him, but He is there with you. In the bible it says, walk by faith and not by sight. (Corinthians 5:7).

Reading the bible is so important because it will help you through life and it teaches you everything. What to do and not to do in life. It will give you answers in today's life, to your questions like, what, when, where, how and why. Although the bible was written centuries ago, guess what, it's so powerful and it still applies to you today because God is the same God today that He was before we were even born. He never changes. We change because we are selfish and self-centered beings especially when He is not a part of your life. Jesus can teach you how to change that! The Bible is like a self-guide on how to handle this life without giving up. You will learn how to be strong when you thought you were so weak, and you will understand that all your help comes from the Lord.

When you finally decide to read your bible and trust God, this will truly help you tremendously because when life seems hard or when you go through difficult situations you will be built up from the Word of God! You will gain hope, faith, wisdom and knowledge but most of all you will understand God has your back and He is here to lift you up and encourage you with the truth and His awesome words.

This is also Gods love story to us! He wants you to know Him and He wants to have a relationship with you. Try your best to spend time with the Lord daily. Read your bible, pray, and seek His presence! You will see the Lord change you if you allow Him too. Also don't be afraid to surrender to Him and give Him your life by being a living sacrifice, basically living for Him and doing what He called you to do in life because reality is we are here in this world for Him and to carry on His work and to do His will. We must be disciples for our King and let people know about His goodness.

3

Fact- Jesus became sin for all of us and He was a man that never sinned, and God loved us so much He gave up His only begotten son for you and me as a sacrifice. Jesus was a sacrifice on the cross and He did not want to die! Jesus cried out to God hoping for another way, but it was God's will because He loved us so much that it had to be done and we were saved from that! That was so beneficial to us because if He would not have died for us, we might not be here today! Now if you ever wonder what true love is, that's it!

Even the grave could not keep Jesus in it! The devil may have thought he won because of Jesus's death but we were blessed with the Holy Spirit after His death. When Jesus was alive, He could only be in one place at a time but now the Holy Spirit can be in everyone at the same time all over the world doing good works! We always get the victory through Jesus Christ our Lord and Savior.

When Jesus died, He rose again on the third day and because of this we get to live again with God. If you are acceptable to God, you will get this opportunity to also be with God, but you must learn how He wants you to be and live as a person while you are still on this earth by reading your bible. God will be proud of you when you start to seek and find who He is and what He is all about.

God will never fail you and He also forgive you for your sins after confessing and repenting them. If you say with your mouth and believe in your heart that Jesus is the son of God and He died on the cross this will get you salvation.

One day there will be a new heaven on earth and the Lord will be with us. There will be no more suffering, pain, or sin! The world will be new, and we will be made new as well (Revelation 21:1-8).

Don't pass the opportunity up to get to know God. The Lord our God will blow your mind and take you on a journey that is full of surprises. After all He created you and knows every detail about you. He knows how many hairs you have on your head and if you are bald, He knows how many hairs you use to have on your head! (Humor)

God will truly bless you if you let Him use you for His purpose and you will be a blessing to other people as well. When we our with our Heavenly Father in heaven, we want to hear job well done son or daughter!! Be quick to repent and sin no more and live a righteous life. When you do this God will wipe away your sins like the sins never took place (Acts 3:19). Wow! What an awesome God we serve!

You may even feel like you are so deep in your sins and that you have done some awful things and you may even feel ashamed about it and think that it is impossible for God to forgive you, but the God I serve transforms people. I know the people that were transformed probably didn't even see it coming! Here is a perfect example, there is a story about a man named King Saul in the Bible, later named Paul who was a murderer. He was a religious man, but he was murdering God's people, and Jesus had to stop him right in his tracks and ask him, why are you doing this to my people and changed his whole life around and when he transformed, that's when his new name Paul came into place. You can read this story in the book and scripture provided (Acts 9 1-22). If God forgave him and so many others, He would forgive you too!

I know life gets tough but when you are on TEAM JESUS you will gain strength and confidence and you will be able to get through a lot of things in this life more smoothly than if you did not have Jesus in your life! Always remember God loves you and you need Him through everything, so just call on His precious name any time! Here is a scripture to recite every day to encourage you. I can do all things through Him who strengthens me (Philippians 4:13).

WHO IS GOD?

Definition: The Creator and ruler of the universe and the source of all moral authority. The supreme being.

God has 3 roles, first He is the father, God. He is also Jesus the son and He is the Holy Spirit who is His spirit, and this is called the Trinity and the Godhead. Reality is all three are really one. They all represent parts of God and who He is. God is powerful so He can be 3 different characters with 3 different functions. He is perfect in every way, and He does not like sin (Psalm 18:30).

The Lord God is Love first (1 John 4:16). He is the truth (John 8:36). He is holy (Leviticus 19:2). He is mighty (Proverbs 23:11). He sees everything all the time and you cannot hide from Him! He is a judge and a redeemer (Isaiah 43:14). He is life, and He gives it (John 14:6). He's our healer, deliverer and provider and He is our way maker (Jeremiah 30:17) (Philippians 4:19) (Psalm 18:2) (Isaiah 43:16). Those are just some of the things that He is to us because He is so much more! He is our High Priest (Hebrews 4:14).

God also has many names and each one has a meaning behind it. Some people called Him Jehovah Jireh which means provider (Genesis 22:14). He was called, Jehovah Rapha which means the Lord who heals (Exodus 15:26). Jehovah Shalom which means the Lord of Peace (Judges 6:24). People cried His name, Abba-Father (Romans 8:15). He is also called I AM (Exodus 3:14) and Alpha and Omega (Revelation 22:13). God has so many names and as you start to dig in your bible you will see and discover His other names. You can't just put 1 name on our King who is awesome and flawless in every way! We as humans only get a few nick names possibly in life but no not our God because He is nothing like us. He is the Supreme Being and reigns on the throne forever! All power is in His hands!

So maybe this will help you understand a little who God is because I know it can be very confusing when you hear God and then Jesus and then you wonder are they the same person and then you might be completely clueless when you hear about The Holy Spirit. This is very important to know all parts of God because they are all important and you must understand the meaning of His divine nature.

When you find out about God it can increase your spiritual level when you learn about all 3. There are people who have gone to church for years and still do not know who The Holy Spirit is. He lives in the saved people and can teach you spiritual things but if you are not interested to learn all about our Heavenly Father you will never know how deep God really is.

God is the Creator, and He created the world and that means everything in it. He created light and night. The sky He created. He parted the waters so there would be land. He created fruit and vegetation from every tree. He made all the animals, big and small and fish and everything in the sea. God created the heavens and the earth in 6 days, but our God needed a break, so He rested on the seventh day and declared that day Holy (Genesis 1:1, 1:3,1:6-8, 1:10-11,1:16,1:20,1:24,1:26,1:27,1:31,2:1-3).

HOW GOD CREATED MAN

The Lord God formed the man from the dust of the ground. He breathed the breath of life into the man's nostrils, and the man became a living person (Genesis 2:7).

When God created Adam, the first man from the bible, He created a beautiful garden with trees and delicious fruit and placed Adam in it. He gave him authority over everything. He gave Adam a job right from the beginning! He had to name all the animals and watch over them (Genesis 2: 8-9) (Genesis 2:15-17) (Genesis 2:18-20).

I believe Adam was not satisfied because he needed a companion that was equal to him and of course God knew how he felt, and He loved Adam. He knew the desire in his heart. He is God! He knows everything. You can't even hide what is in your heart because God knows you so well! One day He created Eve, the first woman. This woman was created from a part of Adam, his rib. God put him in a deep sleep to get his rib and created another creation. Adam was so happy for his new mate! (Genesis 2:21-23).

Can you imagine how Adam felt after seeing all those animals but still not having a companion that resembled him? He could have felt lonely and dissatisfied, but God changed that situation. He probably did not even think he was going to be able to create life too with his wife Eve. He created generations with this special being called woman.

God walked with them as a friend and a father! God is so faithful and loyal. He never betrays us or turn away from us or leaves us! We are the only ones that change because He never does. People can leave the presence of God, but God never leaves us (1 Chronicles 28:20).

HOW SIN STARTED

Definition: an immoral act considered to be a transgression against divine law.

The serpent (a large snake) was the shrewdest of all the wild animals the Lord had made. One day he asked the woman, "Did God really say you must not eat the fruit from any of the trees in the garden?" Of course, we may eat fruit from the trees in the garden, the woman replied" (Genesis 3: 1-2).

Definition

Shrewd: Sharp-witted, Sharp, Intelligent, clever

The devil comes in all kinds of forms to get to you! One day that snake, who is the devil tempted Eve to eat fruit, from a tree. God specifically said do not eat from the tree of life or you will die (Genesis 3:3). Satan lied and said that she would not die and will be like God and be able to know good from evil and then she did it and gave it to her husband Adam to eat as well (Genesis 3:4-5) (Genesis 3:6). Once they ate it their innocence was unveiled, and they realized they were naked and felt shame and sewed fig leaves together themselves to cover up (Genesis 3:7). When this happened, sin entered their lives for being disobedient.

How we raise our children and expect them to obey us is the same way God, our Heavenly Father wants us to obey Him! So, you know how it feels when a person does not obey you or abide by your rules and of course this is not a good feeling. You just want the best for your children and that's exactly how God feels about us! Can you imagine how God feels when you disobey? Ponder on that thought and repent right now if you must.

God was walking in the Garden and then called Adam, but he and his wife were hiding because now they are no longer pure and innocent, and they know they do not have any clothes on because their eyes were opened (Genesis 3:8-12).

THE BLAME GAME

Always take responsibility for your own actions. They started blaming each other! God called man first and asked, where are you? I believe Adam knew better because he was with God first and knew what was expected of him so there was no excuse. God also asked Eve, what have you done, and she blamed the snake (Genesis 3:13). Neither of them is owning up to what they did! Disobedience will cost you! Own up to your faults because a person can't make you do anything. You must respond with your own mouth and physically act on it for it take place. You will have to make it happen! You may be tempted but you make the final decision to put it into play.

PUNISHMENT TIME

When God approached the snake, He told him he will crawl on his belly forever (Genesis 3:14). The woman was punished by having pregnancy pains sharpened while giving birth (Genesis 3:16). The man's punishment was that the ground was cursed, and he would struggle to make a living from it (Genesis 3:17-19). Finally, God had to kick them out of the Garden of Eden because He could not trust them and there was another tree in the garden, the tree of life and if they were to eat from that tree they would live forever.

God made clothes from animal skins for them (Genesis 3:20-21), and Adam was sent out by God to cultivate the ground from which he had been made (Genesis 3:22-23). You see the devil lied and told her that she would gain wisdom and be like God, but the truth is the devil always lies. He is the father of lies and he tried to be higher than God! That is why he is in hell because you can't fool God and he got thrown out of heaven along with some angels that he happened to convince and now they are in hell and will burn forever! (Revelations 12:9)

I know most of the world is blind to the truth, but it is important to know how the world was made and who made you. I know as a child you probably didn't think of who the maker and designer of the world was and just thought we came out of our mother's womb and that's it! But no world! This is bigger and deeper than that. As you get older you get curious, and you can find all the facts in the Holy Bible which is called the Word of God.

It is important to know who the real God is, and His name is Jesus, and nothing can go to the Father without going through the son first because God gave Jesus that authority. Don't you really want to know when you die where you will go?

Also, you have this opportunity to go to heaven because of Jesus's death on the cross and Him dying for us but you can't just get there without making any effort. This is not just an easy and quick trip on the plane, train, or bus we are talking spirituality. You will have to do some work to get to heaven while you are still alive right now. God can't just let you in and let me explain why. God is perfect and we are sinners and yes Jesus saved us from sin, but you will also have to decide if you are going to abide by the instructions and directions from in the bible to live a sinless life. You will go through things on this earth and some people will want to give up but be patient because you will have your time (John 16:33) (James 1:12).

You want to know God was pleased with you on earth and when your flesh is gone, and the blood is not pumping through your veins you will be with God. Will you live in the world and be a part of it or will you live in the world and separate yourself from the worldly ways to be righteous and holy like Jesus Christ our Lord and Savior?

You see reality is that Satan is the ruler of this world (John: 12:31) and he is in hell right now and his judgement is pending because he is going to burn for eternity and you don't want to be a part of that, that is why you must be different and recognize good from bad!

You may have to let some toxic relationships and things go in your life if you are trying to live for God. Make your goal in this life, to be, to get to Heaven. It is worth it! The bottom line is if you take sides with the devil, you are on your way to hell because the bible says sin leads to death but when you let God lead you and you live for Him, your name will be written in the book of life, and you will live forever (Revelation 20:15). So, when you die you will be buried in the grave, but your spirit will live with God forever and eternity (1 John 2:15-17) (1 John 5:18-21).

To walk with God is an honor and a privilege and the wonderful things about our Heavenly Father are endless! Learn about Jesus for yourself and share the goodness about Him with others. This is major so this should be something you want to accomplish on this earth while you are still here.

Don't let this life slow you down by getting distracted and off course. You will face many giants (problems and situations) on earth, but God is right there with you through it all so stay encouraged daily!

God loves you unconditionally so please let that sink down in your entire being and understand that His love will never leave you and there is not one thing that you can do to make Him love you more than He already does.

In life you will make many choices and decisions, but I hope choosing God is a decision that you make more sooner than later and open your heart to Him. Be vulnerable with the Lord because Him guiding you through life will be a path that will keep you on the straight and narrow. Let God show you His truth and His way on how to live in this life and how to walk with Him every day.

Remember live in this world but do not be of this world (Romans 12:1-2). This will make you different and people may think you are weird and strange because your Christian belief of God, Jesus, and The Holy Spirit. Your obedience is something valued by God and not man so a lot of people will not understand you because they may not know the Lord but pray for people and for their understanding and encourage them.

Our real DNA comes from God that is who we originate from, and we are made in the image of our Heavenly Father (Genesis 1:27).

When you do the Lords will, He will be smiling down on you and what a proud Father He will be! This is what you should strive for in life. That should be number one on your list of agendas and goals.

Instead of always looking for a blessing from God be a blessing to Him and that should fulfill you. God is always watching your every move and He looks at the heart to see who you really are (1 Samuel 16:7). Be intentional to do good things every day. You will bless God when you seek Him. It will bring much joy to the Lord that you want to get closer to Him. Think of God for once in your life because He thought of you first! Be selfless not selfish and this will bring joy and it will bless you as well (Ephesians 1:4).

WHO IS JESUS?

Definition- Savior

Jesus was a man not born like you or me. Jesus was conceived by The Holy Spirit. Carried by His young mother Mary who was a virgin. At that time Mary was engaged to a man named Joseph and when pregnancy was learned by them Joseph did not want to have anything to do with her, but an Angel appeared to him in a dream to let him know to not be afraid to take Mary as his wife. The angel said, "she is to have a son and you are to name Him Jesus, for He is to save His people from their sins".

(Matthew 1:18-21)

Fact-Jesus was born in Bethlehem of Judea. (Matthew 2:1)

If Joseph did not listen to the angel, he would have missed out on a very rewarding experience and a blessing! Jesus Christ our Lord and Savior as his very own son. King Jesus is His name awesome in every way! Therefore, you can't fear the things of God and the devil puts that fear in you but guess what the Lord puts faith in you, the very opposite. Joseph had Faith! The bible says For God hath not given us the spirit of fear, but of power, and of love and of a sound mind (2 Timothy 1:7).

God loves us so much that He came from heaven and created Himself through a young woman with His Spirit, to be created as a human being to be born. He came to earth and people were able to experience His greatness and walk with Him as well. He was a man just like you and I. God created a way physically to be with us on earth! He could have stayed on His throne and communicated through His power, through people and His angels but instead He got up close and personal with the people in the world. Jesus was face to face and one on one with humans, imperfect people, our personal Lord and Savior. (Luke 2:11)

Ponder on this: Can you imagine if you were born at the time when Jesus was on this earth, and you crossed His path to talk to Him? How would you feel? What would you say? How would you act? How would you honor him? Although you were not there you still have a chance to do those things right now. Make a list of your answers and talk to God and express your feelings to Him. I'm sure He would love to hear you out. The greatest thing is the Lord always wants to have a relationship with you and it is never too late!

When Jesus got baptized God spoke from Heaven to say how He was pleased with Him and how He loved Jesus very much. Now at that time there were people around and they heard God's voice too! Let me not make this sound so simple because we are talking about God and power here so let me rephrase this, what God did was busted that sky open and His Spirit came down upon Jesus which was The Holy Spirit and at that moment all 3 parts of God was present, God, Jesus, and Holy Spirit (Matthew 3:16-17).

I want to tell you how Jesus was like us. Just how we get tempted by the devil so did He! He was tempted by the devil shortly after His baptism. He had work to do so He went on in the wilderness and didn't eat for 40 days and 40 nights. Jesus was very hungry! The devil tried to get Him to turn stones into bread, but Jesus was wise and had to let him know that man do not live by this physical food alone but by what God says. You see God's food which are the words in the bible will feed your spirit because God is spirit and God's spirit lives in the saved people in this world.

Then the devil took Him to the highest point in Jerusalem and wanted Him to jump! He told Jesus that the angels would save Him. Then the devil tried to throw a scripture at Jesus to try to convince Him, but Jesus had to tell him do not test the Lord your God! Satan, who is the devil took Jesus on a high mountain and showed Him the world and said he would give it to Jesus if He bowed down and worshipped him! Jesus had to let him know to get out of His face and told him you must only worship the Lord your God and serve only Him. Then satan left Jesus! (Matthew 4:1-11)

Jesus did not listen to the devil so that shows you, just because you are tempted does not mean you have to sin. The bible says resist the devil and he will flee from you (James 4:7).

Jesus started His journey to spread the good news and to heal people and to encourage them. He was a very compassionate man and Jesus cared. He didn't want people to be sad, sick, or hungry and if there was something He could do He did it (Matthew 15:32) (Luke 7:13) Matthew 14:14). Jesus was also a faithful man He prayed over everything and knew His Father was going to answer because of His faith. He did not doubt, He was just expecting for whatever He was praying for to be answered by His Father, God. Jesus had so much love for people and just how His Father God loved Him, that is how He loved people (John 15:9).

When Jesus died for us that showed how much He really loved us! (Ephesians 5:2) Jesus was a gentle man but one day He did get angry because He went in the temple, and this was a special place for Him. This is where God was honored. He considered this temple Holy. People were selling animals and doves and making money and He was very upset and made a whip and drove these people out of the temple and Jesus poured out the money they made and overturned those tables in the temple. Jesus told those people to get out of there because this was not going to be a house of merchandise! (John 2:13-16) This was a disgrace! You must be bold when you stand for God because you are a representing Him, so as a believer, follower, and disciple you cannot let people treat God any kind of way!

Jesus is like our middleman, but He is our number one man too. We pray to God, and Jesus pleads our case to the Father but it is important to be obedient so your prayers can be answered. You must learn how to be obedient and righteous to God like Jesus and to abide by His commandments and rules and through your actions and words it will show if you truly belong to God.

First, you must believe in Jesus Christ. Follow and copy Him (Ephesians 5:1). You also must stay in fellowship with Him (John 15:12). After all, when Jesus died, He left His spirit to live in us so it is important that we look like Him daily so people will recognize that He is in you and doing a great work through you! People will see how you have changed, and they will notice the Lord's light is shining through you. You too are here on earth to help, heal and save people just like Jesus (John 14:15-18).

WHO IS THE HOLY SPIRIT?

DEFINITION

(In Christianity) the third person of the trinity; God as spiritually active in the world.

The Holy Spirit is the third person in the trinity-Godhead. This is the order, God, Jesus, Holy Spirit

The Holy Spirit lives inside of you and helps you through life. He is also the truth because The Holy Spirit is God's Spirit as explained previously. God communicates through The Holy Spirit to speak to humans through your spirit that each person has inside of them. The Holy Spirit will allow you to experience God's power that will help you to discern the spiritual things that a human mind cannot understand. It's God's power in you! This is an awesome part of God to experience.

A lot of Christians in this world do not take this big step to even get a chance to see and feel this part of God because they are afraid or are just comfortable where they are in their walk with the Lord and wont attempt to go any further. I am telling you from my walk with God and experiencing The Holy Spirit living inside of me is a blessing, and I don't ever want God's Spirit to leave me! The Holy Spirit gives me confirmation and from Him living inside of me I know God really loves me so much because He is a part of me, and He resides inside of me. It is important to take the extra step to get baptized with The Holy Spirit because you will experience a spiritual connection. This is a touch from God to you.

Some people may not know but after you accept Jesus in your heart and get baptized in the water then the next baptism is with The Holy Spirit, and everyone will have a different experience (Matthew 3:11). When I got baptized with The Holy Spirit shortly after a language came out of me which is called tongues. This language is between you and God. I do not know what I am saying but God does. This was proof to me that something was happening in the spirit! (1 Corinthians 14:1-2)

Before Jesus left this earth, He told His disciples that He was going to ask God for another helper on this earth. He probably did not want them to feel abandoned after He died as well. God never leaves us, but they were used to physically seeing Him. This helper to be sent is Jesus but in another form (John 14:26-27).

When Jesus was on the earth, He could only be in one place at a time but when The Holy Spirit came after Jesus death it allowed Jesus in spirit form to be in everyone at the same time. This was awesome for us because if Jesus did not die, we would not have this power from the Lord! When Jesus was on earth some people came in Jesus's presence to ask what they wanted of Him but now we can do the same works Jesus did and we are His disciples, and we can operate in His power too (John 14:12).

This is what Jesus said, and I will ask the Father, and He will give you another helper(Comforter, Advocate, Intercessor-Counselor, Strengthener, Standby), to be with you forever-the Spirit of Truth, whom the world cannot receive[and take to its heart] because it does not see Him or know Him, but you know Him because He(The Holy Spirit) remains with you continually and will be in you(John 14:16-17).

WHO IS THE DEVIL?

DEFINITION

(In Christian and Jewish belief) the chief evil spirit; Satan

First, he is our enemy! There is nothing good about him at all. He ruined his opportunity with the Lord because he thought he could outsmart God and was thrown out of Heaven! (Isaiah 14:12-15) He knows we win because we always have the victory through our Lord and Savior Jesus Christ, but he still tries to sliver his ugly head into your life to see how far he can take you to the pit and if he can kill you believe me, he will!

His Goal is to steal, kill and destroy and he is on a mission to get these things done on this earth! (John 10:10) Now, remember what I told you we win so you better believe you can fight against him by knowing the word of God and that is the bible. Let me explain, the words in the bible is your weapon and you use it by fighting with scripture against the devil. It is like when someone gets shot and the bullet hits a person and that's exactly what it does to Satan and his demons. In the bible it says to put on the whole armor of God so that you can stand against him (Ephesians 6:11).

See you may think that this is the only world but there is also a spiritual world we cannot see. You can't see the devil, but he works through people. That is why so many bad and evil things happen and people think it's just the person that they see that's doing evil works. The devil works through people to hurt people! In the bible it says we don't wrestle against flesh and blood but against spiritual forces of evil (Ephesians 6:12).

The Devil also known as satan was sent to this earth. He is also known as the prince of the air (Ephesians 2:2). We belong to God, but the world belongs to the devil that is why you can't just go with the way of the world and do whatever the world does because it is not of Jesus (1 John 5:19). Satan is always trying to distract you so that you won't believe and follow Jesus (2 Corinthians 4:4). Therefore, you must always be ready because one wrong move and he might attack you! (1 Peter 5:8-9)

I know a lot of people think the devil is this ugly red horned guy, but he comes in so many disguises you cannot pin one on him because he is a trickster! (2 Corinthians 11:14)

At one time he was very beautiful, made with all the finest jewels and he was anointed at one point and was even blameless but then unrighteousness was found in him! (Ezekiel 28:13-19) The bottom line is he is no good for you and if you follow him you will go to hell! If you have some of his characteristics right now, then that is where you are headed if you don't change. He is a murderer and a liar, and he is of every bad thing you can imagine! He is a deceiver and a father of all lies (John 8:44).

See, you must be careful in this life with the things that you see, hear, and do because it may be bad for you and that's when you know that it is of the devil. The bible says the lamp of the body is the eye (Luke 11:33-36). Bad things can settle down inside of you and get comfortable. The flesh never gets enough! It is never satisfied and has a heavy appetite so you can get caught up in your sin(s) and will not stop and if you don't stop that means you want to keep on sinning because you want more of whatever sin you are idolizing.

When you keep feeding on the things of the devil, those desires can get heavier, and the sin gets deeper, and they are turned into strongholds on you and in your life. It's like the devil's demons got a grip on you! Now, God does not want that for your life, so you must fight for your life because the devil is coming every second of the day! He may leave for a moment, but he will always come back! You must be ready for him! When he does come you will know what to do, throw a bible verse at him, then another and another one, pray and put him all the way down!

You already have the victory through Jesus but there will be many temptations and tests in life whether you are having a good or bad day, so you must be strong and know how to handle his tricks, schemes, and foolery! He wants to destroy you!

One way that the devil can attack you is through your mind. He will have you believing lie after lie. He will have you believe that you are not good enough, you are incompetent, or you are not pretty enough!! God did not say these things, so you know it's a lie!

When God created humans, He said it was good! We all look different but we are made in the image of God so it does not matter who may think you are not beautiful because you are beautiful, and you are made from a King, and you resemble God and that is beauty! Don't let the devil fool you!

Satan also attacks you through people. Sometimes it can be the closest person to you and the person can have an attitude towards you for no reason or start an argument or talk about you behind your back or to your face. That's why it is important for you to recognize when the devil is using someone to attack you and the sad thing is the person who is doing the harm to you don't even know that they are being used by this evil spirit to get to you. That is why we must continually pray for people to come to the Lord so people can know the truth and follow the real God, Jesus!

Truth is, anytime that you let the devil get to you he is stealing from you! He can steal your peace and your joy, and those things belong to you, given to you from Jesus.

He can steal your money when you use it on things that are not of God. It could be gambling, material items, drugs and so many other worldly things and it is sad because the world takes pleasure in so many of these bad things and many more. The reality is that you should ask God how to spend your money because this way you know it will be what He wants you to do but people do what they want and use money on things that are not of God. So much money is being spent on unnecessary things, things that the flesh wants, and the flesh is very weak it wants what it wants and when it wants because it is never satisfied.

We all have sinned but one day you must stand up and say enough is enough and stop letting the devil run your life and fight back against him instead of being so quick to give into sin because sin is of the devil (1 John 3:8). The bible says sin leads to death (Romans 6:23) (James1:15).

God will never tempt you to be sinful and if you have ever blamed God for the devil's wrongdoing, please ask God for forgiveness because we serve a great and loving God and that is not in his nature. The bible says that you are drawn by your own desires and when the desire is conceived, it gives birth to sin and then when it is full grown births into death (James 1:12-15).

When you keep on sinning after Jesus already set you free you are still putting yourself back in slavery to sin and it is like crucifying Jesus repeatedly (Hebrews 6:4-6). Also, when you stop the sin and go back to it the bible says it is worse than before and comes back seven times stronger (Matthew 12:43-45).

You will have to make a choice and believe me choosing Jesus is the right one. God will always have your back, and the devil will come sneaking around to see if he can destroy or devour you but eventually, he has to leave you (James 4:7) (2 Thessalonians 3:3).

One major thing people don't know is if you do not forgive people, God will not forgive you! (Matthew 6:14-15) I know it is hard to forgive people when they have stabbed you in the back, betrayed, lied or hurt you really bad but don't hinder what you have with the Lord over someone else's ignorance (Hebrews 12:14-15). Forgive them and let God deal with them appropriately. Let God fight your battle! (Exodus 14:14)

People are going to let you down in this life, but God will never do that and that's why you always trust in Him more than people. God forgave you over and ever again and still is forgiving you and if we were made like Him, we must forgive too! Stay encouraged daily and always keep the Lords truth in your heart and in your everyday living. Don't let the devil deceive you because that's what he wants (2 Corinthians 11:3). The bible says what the devil meant for bad God can turn it around for your good and that is a blessing right there (Genesis 50:20).

Have faith in God when a bad situation comes up and trust God that He will give you something better, even if you don't see the result right away just believe in Jesus with all your heart! He will make it right!

(See scriptures on unforgiveness; 2 Corinthians 2:10-11,1 John 1:9, Matthew 18:21-22, Leviticus 19:17-18)

Ponder on this: What if when Jesus was on earth, you were on the earth too and you were spending some time with Him physically, in the flesh. Would you be able to act how you act right now around Him or would you be able to live how you live daily today in His presence? Would you be able to say or do what you want with Him right there, you know you being how you are everyday? If you could not and are ashamed of how you are living, then you are not living for the Lord, you are living for the devil.

When you are living for God, you won't be ashamed because you are living a righteous life. If you are living for God, great job! Keep enduring this life and doing right by God because you will be rewarded by Your Heavenly Father. If you are living an unrighteous life today and you are reading this book you still have time right at this moment to repent and start living for Him today! Don't let the devil talk you out of it because time is running out! The bible says be quick to repent and sin no more (Acts 3:19).

WHAT IS FAITH?

DEFINITION

Faith-Complete trust or confidence in someone or something

To know God, you will have to believe in Him first. To please God, you must have faith (Hebrews 11:6). Faith is believing in things that are hoped for but not actually seeing it (Hebrews 11:1). A lot of people in the bible had faith because they believed God was real and they trusted God.

There is a story about a man named Abraham who was married to a lady name Sarah, and they conceived at nearly 100 years old. God told her that she would have a baby and God promised Abraham earlier in the story that he would have a son. Unfortunately, Sarah got a little impatient and took the situation in her own hands and instructed her servant to sleep with her husband to have a baby! This was a problem because Sarah was the one that needed to conceive, Abraham's wife so this was her idea not God's (Genesis 16:1-4). You must keep the faith, be patient and wait on God! Eventually Sarah got pregnant and her and Abraham had a son named Isaac (Genesis 21:1-7).

God is faithful and He is going to do what He said when He say it is time. Abraham and Sarah did have faith in God because they had to be intimate to have a baby and I am sure at that age they may have not been feeling up to the task, but they did it because they believed. They just got a little impatient in the waiting process. Always wait on God so that you can receive the blessing that He has for you!

When you look at the beautiful things in the world like the sky, trees, and the sun you know a man did not make those things (Genesis 1:1-31). There is no way a human can create the sky or the sun it is impossible! You would not even be able to wrap your mind around it because the question would be, how, and there is no possible answer because a human could not ever create the things that God created. When you think about that, that should make you have faith because you won't have a clue on how it got there. I can only believe God did it with a command and that started with a word in the beginning of the world when it was created (Hebrews 11:3).

When you get closer to God, He will speak to you through your spirit and His spirit that lives inside of you. You will learn to understand when He is telling you to do something, and you will also believe by faith that He is speaking to you.

I know when I see homeless people on the street, I help them. I may share the goodness of Jesus and then talk to them and give them some money because the word says faith alone is not enough, unless it produces good deeds and if not, it is useless (James 2:17). The bible also says faith is dead without good works (James 2:26).

So along with your faith you will have to do some things too because when you act it proves that you are not just saying I will pray for you, but you are also actually showing a person that you want to help! With your works this may increase a person's faith and that may help them believe in the prayer that you may leave with them. This may also increase their belief in the Lord (James 2:15-17).

Personal Testimony

Here is one of my personal testimonies on what my faith did and how God showed up for me! He heard my prayer and came right on time!

One day my husband and I were on the freeway going home and his truck stopped! My husband was very frustrated and stated that there were a couple of times he got stuck on the freeway and nobody stopped to see if he needed any help!

He felt this was just a replay of what happened before being stranded and him having to get himself out of the situation! In his mind he probably felt like we will just have to figure it on our own! I said to my husband, "Don't worry someone will come and help us". Now my faith was untouchable and no matter what you said against what I believed; I knew God was going to do it! God was going to get us out of this bad situation! You could not even shake me because I had faith in my God that I serve! I didn't care how it looked I just knew in my heart something good was going to happen!

My husband was a little agitated, but I was calm. I said a soft whispered prayer and waited patiently for someone to come to our rescue because I knew God was going to show up! I didn't know when, but I knew it would be soon. Only just a few minutes later someone pulled up to help us, then minutes after that another person came and then a third person, but the last person saw that we were being helped and kept going.

Once we finally started back driving on the freeway, I looked at my husband and said, "I told you that God would do it!" I said this with joy and confidence to my husband.

I felt the love my Heavenly Father showed me that day because He showed up and showed all the way out because numerous people came to our rescue on that same freeway my husband had bad experiences on before but that day, I felt so much love from God and that moment was very rewarding.

Sometimes you just don't want to say, I told you so, but I had to brag on this God of mine. He is so awesome in every way, and He thought of me because He cares, and not only for me but for my husband too!

If you believe and have faith, God will show you some amazing things! God is the only one that can do the impossible if you will just believe and trust Him every day of your life! (Luke 1:37)

God is full of surprises and goes beyond what we can imagine. You just have faith and keep it!

WHAT IS A MIRACLE?

Definition

A surprising and welcome event that is not explicable by natural or scientific laws and is therefore considered to be the work of a divine agency

I feel only God can do a miracle and sometimes He works through people to get it done. Jesus was performing miracles when He was on the earth, and He is still the same today as He was thousands and thousands of years ago. He is still performing miracles to this day. He is continually healing people!

A doctor may give a person a deadly diagnosis but suddenly, the results are not life threatening anymore or if someone was told they were barren but eventually gets pregnant or even coming out of a coma or any situation that you knew of that should not have been a success, but it was because God is with you, and he performed a miracle for you! God always wants you healed. The Lord will get in the fire with you!

There is a great story, a true story how the Lord was with these three Hebrew boys that refuse to bow down to any other than God and was penalized and thrown into a hot, burning furnace but Jesus got in the fire with them, and He protected them and not even a hair on their heads were burned! You can read about this in (Daniel 3 8-30) it goes with faith too because sometimes you will have to believe for the miracle to happen.

When Jesus walked the earth, He did plenty of miracles! There is a story in the bible about this lady and to me she had strong faith! She believed for this miracle of healing without seeing, feeling, or knowing what was going to happen but she believed with all her heart, and she acted on it! She believed if she could get close enough to Jesus, she could just touch the bottom of His clothes when He walked by and that she would be healed! That is exactly what happened too! Jesus healed her of twelve years of hemorrhaging because she had faith and believed. Jesus even told her that her faith has made her well and she was healed at that very moment! (Matthew 9:20-22)

Here is another example of great faith! This situation was approached with no fear just faith! These men were just expecting the miracle. This story is about two blind me who followed Jesus one day and yelled to the Lord to have mercy on them! Jesus asked them first by testing their faith did they believe that He could make them see again and they both answered yes, and Jesus touched their eyes but because of their faith they were able to see. (Matthew 9:27-28)

God can do some miraculous things with you as well. I know sometimes you may feel like God can't change you or a loved one's situation from being toxic, sick, homeless, broke, or even breaking a drug addiction and you may even say to yourself that this is going to take a miracle, but God can do anything and can heal everything! As you can see, He performs miracles! He can make it right! The Lord God can heal any situation. He is blessing people every second of the day! God is a miracle worker! His mighty power and His grace and mercy overpowers us and His unconditional love is enough to make you right. If you follow his lead, He can help you turn your sinful life into a righteous one, but you must give Him a chance and your life depends on it!

I know you may have heard of the stories from the bible how Jesus walked on water (see Matthew 14:24-32) or how He fed over five thousand people that followed Him with only five loaves of bread and two fish (Matthew 14:13-21) or when He performed His very first miracle turning water into wine (John 2:1-11).

These true stories and so many other stories in the bible will blow your mind! We are truly blessed to have a King that wants to be a part of our lives, to help, to heal and to make you whole. Jesus died for you and loves you so much!

Jesus paid the price for us all and that alone is worth picking up the bible to read how wonderful and awesome He is and getting to know Him. Give Him the chance that He deserves because He took a chance on you and loved you enough to suffer for you on that cross!

Jesus was still asking God His Father to forgive people, although His own people denied Him! Also accepting a person into the kingdom on the other side of Him being crucified as well. He was suffering so much pain, with nails in His hands and feet, blood dripping from His body and thirst that He needed but never quenched! He was still thinking of mankind even when He was taking His last breaths!

Shortly after He was also pierced in His side with a sharp weapon to confirm His death! No words can explain our loving and unselfish Savior! We must give Him the praise, honor, glory, and thanks!

Miracle Testimonies

1st Testimony- When I was born, I was premature weighing 3 pounds and 7 ounces. I was a 7-month baby, and the doctors told my parents that I was not going to live. My mom said that my sister would pray for me, and she was only five years old.

I didn't have a name right away they just called me baby Davis, and truth is the doctors did not expect me to pull through, but you see, glory to God, I am alive, and I made it because of prayer and hope and because God wanted me here, on earth, alive and free and YES it was a miracle! If I was not here today, I would not have been able to write this book to tell you all these wonderful things about the Lord, but my fate is only in God's hands, and I am so thankful and grateful for my life! Thank you, Jesus!

2nd Testimony- One day My husband, both daughters and I were traveling from New York back home in our car. We were having a great time singing, talking about the Lord, and just enjoying each other's company on our journey. Well, we were driving at a pace with the flow of traffic. As we looked ahead in the rearview mirror, we saw two cars speeding up so fast behind us! We saw a car stopped in front of us in our lane but the cars behind us could not see the stopped car ahead to know to stop or slow down. We could not get over to another lane because those cars were going fast and with the flow of traffic as well. We came up so quick to the car in front of us that if we stopped the cars behind us were going to hit our car and then we would have hit the car in front of us!

All I could do is brace myself because we came up so fast and the cars behind us were going so fast it was going to be impossible to hit the brakes without us crashing into the stopped car in front of us. God showed up right on time leading the two cars behind us in a ditch off the freeway! It was God that saved us! I started thanking and praising God for keeping us safe! With my physical eyes all I could see ahead was something horrible about to happen, but the Lord protected us! I said out loud to my family, that had to be the angels lifting those cars up to prevent from hitting us! My husband and I were speechless yet grateful for this blessing for our family!

PROMISES FROM GOD

Definition

A declaration or assurance that one will do a particular thing will happen.

Assure someone that one will definitely do, give, or arrange something, undertake, or declare that something will happen

Here are some promises from God that you can receive. You must believe and receive them in your heart. God has promises for you daily and if you don't seek the Lord how will you know what belongs to you. The Lord is with you every day because He said that He would never leave you. There are times when you will go through trials and tribulations in your life. You may even feel overwhelmed, weak, tired, and feel like you don't want to go on or push anymore but the Lord is your strength! Let God fight your battles because He said that He would, and you don't have to feel alone or defeated because you have the victory through Jesus, and He already won the battle! Be encouraged!

I know sometimes when you pray for something you may not see results right away and start to feel hopeless, so you keep repeating the prayer just in case God did not hear you the first times because honestly that is what you think, but God is not hard of hearing, He heard you the first time! He hears your prayers. Sometimes you will have to be still and trust God even when it feels uncomfortable but keep faith alive and expect Him to show up any moment and be ready and trust in His timing because He knows what is best for you!

The Lord wants you to be happy and He wants you to always prosper because He said it in His word. He has a plan, and it is not your plan so when you take His route you will succeed.

I know there are times when you may worry about some things or situations, and you can't sleep, and your mind is constantly going but God said that He will give you peace. The reason why is because God has your best interest at heart and has a solution to your life and the number one thing is that He loves you!

This is a list of promises from God to you:

Healing Promises—

(Jeremiah 17:14) Heal me, O Lord, and I shall be healed; Save me and I shall be saved, for you are my praise.

(3 John 1:2) Beloved, I pray that you may prosper in all things and be in health, just as your soul prospers.

(Luke 6:19) And the whole multitude sought to touch him, for power went out from Him, and healed them all.

(Psalm 103:2-3) Bless the Lord O my soul, and forget not all his benefits: Who forgives all of your iniquities, Who heals all your diseases.

(Isaiah 53:5) But He was wounded for our transgressions, He was bruised for our iniquities; The chastisement for our peace was upon Him, And by His stripes we are healed.

Family Promises-

(Proverbs: 14:26) In the fear of the Lord there is strong confidence, And His children will have a place of refuge.

(Psalm 22:30) A posterity shall serve Him. It will be recounted of the Lord to the next generation.

(Isaiah 54:17) No weapon formed against you shall prosper, and every tongue which rises against you in judgement, you shall condemn.

(Psalm 90:16-17) Let Your work appear to your servants, And your Glory to their children. And let the beauty of the Lord our God be upon us and establish the work of our hands for us; Yes, establish the work of our hands.

(Psalm 102:28) The children of Your servants will continue, and their descendants will be established before you.

Promises for your life

(Ephesians 2:10) For we are His workmanship, created in Christ Jesus, for good works which God prepared beforehand that we shall walk in them.

(Jeremiah 29:11) For I know the thoughts that I think toward you, says the Lord, thoughts of peace and not of evil, to give you future and a hope.

(Isaiah 41:10) Fear not, for I am with you; Be not dismayed for I am your God. I will strengthen you, yes, I will help you, I will uphold you with My righteous right hand.

(Joshua 1:9) Have I not commanded you? Be strong and of good courage; do not be afraid, nor be dismayed, for the Lord your God is with you wherever you go.

(Hebrews 10:23) Let us hold fast the confession of our hope without wavering, for He who promised is faithful.

When you start seeking God by reading your bible and praying you will see that the Lords promises are endless. He has a lot in store for you when you are a child of God.

To be a child of God is a promise as well and you should be walking in His truth and standing for Him every single day.

You will have to believe Jesus is the son of God and that He died for you and then after confessing this truth start following the Lords way, and you will receive your salvation through Jesus Christ and that is how you will be a part of God's family!

Do your best to get in Gods family! He wants you to come to Him, but you will have to take that first step to enter the

Kingdom! God is waiting on you! Take a leap of faith and trust Him with everything you got! You will gain everlasting life by believing and following Jesus.

If you do not believe in Jesus, but you die and then go to hell because you followed the world and didn't make any effort to try to seek him, you will miss out on a new spiritual life of greatness with the Lord and if that happens, it will be too late for you to be saved and to go to Heaven!! Hell is not a place you want to go!

Instead of just living life for today and pleasing your fleshly and worldly needs, you must start thinking about eternity and that will come after this life on earth! Don't be a fool! (Psalm 14:1) This world will soon go away! (1 John 2:17) Make this the smartest move you will ever make by choosing life with God!

SUMMING IT ALL UP

To sum this book up is to understand that we were created from God, The Father and Jesus came to save us from the sins of the world. Jesus died for us on the cross and shed His Blood for us (Matthew 26:28) (1 Peter 1:19-21).

A piece of Him was sent to us to take His place spiritually instead of physically and He is called The Holy Spirit (John 14:26).

God is our Father and Creator, and He is above all and comes first. God is our everything! He protects you and loves you unconditionally. God is who we pray to and through Jesus your prayers are delivered. God is the Boss, and everything must go through Him for approval whether it is spiritual or carnal.

Jesus is our Lord and Savior. He was born as a human being and has gone through things in life on earth just like us. He can relate to us because He was like us. This is God in human form representing Himself as the Son of God!

Jesus died for us and was sacrificed for us on the cross. He became sin for the world and when He called out to God on the cross God did not acknowledge Him because Jesus took the place for our sins and God does not like sin because it is unholy. God is so Holy that you cannot be in his presence if you have sin in you so right now you must try to be sinless and pure. Being pure is not mixed with anything including this world.

You still have time to repent for your wrong doings and do your best to become righteous and blameless so that one day when it is your time you can be in the presence of the Lord because you too can become holy like God.

When Jesus died and rose again, we gained this blessing to live with God for eternity, but you will have to live God's way, and this must be a lifestyle that you live every day (1 John 5:20). When you die, your spirit man will rise, and the flesh will die. (Ecclesiastes 12:7) Your spirit lives in your body and that is your righteous man.

47

Understand your spirit was with God first. He formed you into your mothers wound. You will go back to your original creation and when you are with God, He is going to give you a new heavenly body (Philippians 3:20-21).

One day Jesus will come back for His people, His righteous and holy ones (Mark 13:32-37).

I know this is a lot of information and I want you to know the truth, but you will have to find out who God is on your own. You will have to read your bible and seek God to find out.

There are so many wonderful and all true stories in the bible. God's word will really open your eyes and show you how wonderful, powerful, and awesome God is (Nehemiah1:5) (Job 37:22) (Psalm 66:5).

Along the journey you will have a lot of encouragement from other Christians.

You might read devotional's, blogs, go on websites or go on social media to hear other people's testimonies and journey. People may even share the Word of God but never get so comfortable with just hearing about God through others because you must find out who He is and what He has planned for you on your own.

You want to gain knowledge about Him so you will learn the truth for yourself and if anyone was to speak falsely about the Lord you will know the truth because you have been doing your studying and research from the Word of God. God will speak to you just like He speaks through and to other people (Jeremiah 33:3).

Jesus paid the price for you so that you can have salvation so take ownership over what was given to you on the account of Jesus blood.

Living for God comes with a new everything. A new mind, attitude, and new actions. It is like being reborn because that's exactly what it is. This is a new you!

You must be different if you ever want to enter into His Glory. You want to get to Heaven and be with God not just slide in and barely have made it!

Jesus fought and prayed for us and pleads our case to the Father (Romans 8:34). Jesus goes to the Father on our behalf (Hebrews 7:25). He feels pain and pity for mankind.

To be in the presence of God, you will have to be holy and righteous.

I always say that I want to be in all of God's Glory when I go to heaven! Do your best to start living a blameless life right now. Don't let the world have power over you because you are the Righteousness of God and take a stand for who you are! (2 Corinthians 5:21)

If you haven't accepted Jesus, be sure to confess Him as Lord because this will save you and this is the will of God. God called us all to be righteous and Holy, but it all starts with obedience and God has called for this as well. If you didn't know who you were through Christ, now you know and as you grow with God you will learn that you are so much more.

The Holy Spirit will help you through life. The Holy Spirit will show you the way, prompt you on decisions, soothe and comfort you. The Holy Spirit is loyal, truthful and is your friend.

When you make decisions in life The Holy Spirit is with you always. God's spirit will rest in you and upon you and when you allow Him to take His place in you be sure to take good care of Him by not grieving the Holy Spirit (Ephesians 4:30-32).

You also must clean up the bad in you because as I mentioned God can't be around unholiness and make His spirit welcome in you and in your heart!

It is important to know your true identity and the truth about the Lord.

Ponder on this-

When you physically eat food, this brings nourishment and strength to your physical body but to feed your spirit man that's inside of you, you must read your bible to feed it and as you gain wisdom and knowledge you will get full (Jeremiah 15:16). Your spirit will grow stronger and wiser. Ask God to show you how to get more spiritual because this is the Power of God working in you and you can operate in some amazing things for the Lord. He has called us all to be Holy so go all the way with God so He can truly get the full benefit of working through you! (1 Thessalonians 4:7-8)

Do not let the devil lie to you, mislead you or destroy you anymore! (John 10:10) You still have a chance because you are still alive, and the devil didn't kill you, so God still has a plan for your life. Set yourself free through Jesus Christ (John 8:36) (Galatians 5:1).

No matter how many sins you have committed, admit them through repentance right away, don't wait because you might forget. God will wipe your sins away. He will make the slate clean as if you have never done them at all because He loves you so much! (1 John 1:10) (Hebrews 8:12) He is a forgiving God!

God is not like a human that will continuously throw your mistakes and all the bad things that you have done back in your face to make you feel the pain, shame, and guilt again. God is your only judge! (Isaiah 33:22) (2 Corinthians 5:10)

God may chastise you when you are wrong, but He will also forgive you. Make it right today with you and God by turning away from your sins. Honor God not just with words but with your heart! No other God can set you free through Jesus only He has the power to do that!

Rest in God, He will forgive you and that is a fact. Don't worry about how you or the situation may look or how you may feel, just believe by faith that you are forgiven by God and go ahead and forgive yourself and be free!

I hope this book has helped you to understand who God, Jesus and The Holy Spirit are, and God does not want you to be confused if you are or ever were. Take your time with God. He deserves your praise, your undivided attention and fellowship!

There are so many different versions of the bible. The words may be slightly different, but the meaning is the same because the bible was inspired by the Holy Spirit. (2 Timothy 3:16)

Here is some examples-King James (KJV), English Standard (ESV), New Living Translation (NLT), Amplified (AMPC), New International (NIV) and the Message (MSG). Please use the best one for you to study from.

God is not hard to understand and love. When you are truly hungry and sincere for Him, you will be willing to learn about Him. He knows you and loves you very much so take the time to get to know Him! (John 15:12-13)

Let me leave you with one last scripture so you can sit on, stand on and meditate on.

(1 John 2:15-17)

Do not love this world or the things that it offers you, for when you love the world, you do not have the love of the Father in you. For the world offers only craving for physical pleasure, a craving for everything we see, and pride in our achievements and possessions. These are not from the Father but are from this world. And the world is fading away, along with everything that people crave. But anyone who does what pleases God will live forever.

KNOWLEDGE FOR YOUR MIND

It is good to be around people who are on the same path as you. The truth is you will have to leave some people behind on your walk with God because everyone is not healthy for you! You will have to pray for people and love them from a distance because your walk can be interrupted because of temptation if you are still with people who are not following the Lord. You may think you are strong enough, but the flesh is weak, and you can be easily influenced and fall back in the sinful lifestyle you lived before accepting Jesus and following His path.

People who walk the path of God like you will help you along the way by encouraging you, praying with you and lifting you up. They will also check on you and hold you accountable for the things that concern God to make sure you are staying on the straight and narrow path. When times get tough you will have the ones that are on this journey as well to talk to and turn to and lean on.

All the believers of God are called the body of Christ, which is one body and that's what we make up because there is one Jesus Christ. Now in this body we all have different functions and parts to play in this body (1 Corinthians 12:12-31).

Here is an example. A human body has many parts in it to make up this one body and all the parts operate differently because of how it functions in the body, but it is still one body and to make this part of the body work it must have all the right parts to do it so that it will function properly. That is how The Body of Christ is, we have different functions and roles in this body for it to operate correctly. You must make sure you are doing your part as a believer in the body so that the entire body can operate properly to get the will of God done in this earth.

As you get closer to God, special gift or gifts will be released into you and this gift(s) is not just for you it is to help lift and encourage other people because you are trying to get people to believe in God so that they too can be part of the Kingdom one day. God really needs you just like you need Him! He needs you to do the work in the earth for Him and the only way that He can get His will done is through people. So as a believer you better start convincing people and sharing all the good things about the Lord and not just being silent in the world. Be bold for God! God did not put you here on earth to not stand for Him.

There is a lot of work that needs to be done by the believers of Jesus Christ. We are the disciples! You might as well start winning people for God right now and doing the work He needs you to do on this earth because when you do get to Heaven that is what you will be doing serving the King.

After going through this Holy internship, one day will be the graduation and when it is your time to go to Heaven you will be working for God forever and you will have all the qualifications and degrees with you!

Remember, this stuff on earth does not matter because it will disappear. If you are idolizing money, jewelry, cars, or fancy clothes or whatever your flesh is desiring, it will go away one day but God will never disappear. He will be with you in Heaven and earth so start to get to know the things of God and Heaven right now and allow Him to bring you the happiness that you need instead of these senseless things that you want! These things cant save you, only God can!

Use your time wisely because it will run out and you don't know exactly when so the best thing you can do today is start using your time for the Lord because then you know when it runs out you will be with the one who loves you and cares the most, God!

The bible says regarding gifts: (Ephesians 4:11-13)

Now these are the gifts that Christ gave to the church: the apostles, the prophets, the evangelists, and the pastors and teachers. Their responsibility is to equip God's people to do His work and build up the church, the body of Christ. This will continue until we all come to such unity in our faith and knowledge of God's Son that we will be mature in the Lord, measuring up to the full and complete standard of Christ.

10 Commandments

Here are the commandments that God instructed for His people to follow when He brought them out of slavery from Egypt and He then wrote them on 2 tablets and added nothing else.

Exodus 20:1(ESV) reads: I am the Lord your God, who brought you out of the land of Egypt, out of the house of slavery.

The Bible has the old and the New Testament. This was the law in the old because of the transgressions but once Jesus came to the earth this was no longer in place.

Today, we live in the new and it is your faith in Jesus Christ that matters. He is the true law and the only way to live. He gave us life because of His death! The bible says the righteous should live by faith (Galatians 3:11-29).

These commands are like an example and although we are not under this law anymore these are some of the things that you should still not do! God expects us to live holy and righteous lives until the day we die. There are no exceptions and if you have done these things and are still doing these things then you need to turn away right now!

You see time is very precious and you don't know when your time will run out on this earth! Every day that you wake up, you have a chance to change your mindset and transform into who God truly destined you to be. If you seek Him, He will be there to guide you and spiritually hold your hand along the way.

God's grace and mercy has given each person a chance and there is nothing you can do on this earth to earn it because this is a blessing from the Lord! He saved us and felt compassion for us. (2 Chronicles 30:9)

There was a time when God wiped out the world and every animal and everything in it! God only found 1 righteous man, Noah in the whole earth.

When Jesus died, God had mercy on us, and Jesus was that sin for us! (Genesis 6: 5-8)

1 You shall have no other gods before me.

2 You shall not make for yourself a carved image, or any likeness of anything that is in heaven above, or that is in the earth beneath, or that is in the water under the earth. You shall not bow down to them or serve them, for I the Lord your God am a jealous God, visiting the iniquity of the fathers on the children to the third and the fourth generation of those who hate me, but showing steadfast love to thousands of those who love me and keep my commandments.

3 You shall not take the name of the Lord your God in vain, for the Lord will not hold him guiltless who takes His name in vain.

4 Remember the Sabbath day, to keep it holy. Six days you shall labor, and do all your work, but the seventh day is a Sabbath to the Lord your God. On it you shall not do any work, you, or your son, or your daughter, your male servant, or your female servant, or your livestock, or the sojourner who is within your gates. For in six days the Lord made heaven and earth, the sea, and all that is in them, and rested on the seventh day. Therefore, the Lord blessed the Sabbath day and made it holy.

5 Honor your father and your mother, that your days may be long in the land that the Lord your God is giving you.

6 You shall not murder.

7 You shall not commit adultery.

8 You shall not steal.

9 You shall not bear false witness against your neighbor.

10 You shall not covet your neighbor's house; you shall not covet your neighbor's wife, or his male servant, or his female servant, or his ox, or his donkey, or anything that is your neighbor's.

PRAYER TO ACCEPT JESUS CHRIST

This is a prayer to accept Jesus as your personal Lord and Savior. If you want to get on the right path with God here is an opportunity to be a part of God's family by confessing Jesus is Lord and to allow God to be Lord over your life. This is your time! If you are serious about Jesus because He is serious about you say this prayer with all your heart and start believing, trusting, and surrendering to God every day. The Lord welcomes you with open arms so come as you are and partner with God to transform you into a beautiful new you!

Dear Lord-

I come to you today with all my heart. I believe you are God and Jesus is your precious son. I believe that Jesus died on the cross for my sins and rose again on the third day. I repent of all my sins and would like to be a new person with your help. I accept Jesus as my Lord and Savior. I ask Him to come into my life today and teach me how to get to know Him and to direct my steps and my path to serve Him. I invite Jesus into my heart today and to show me how to be a good disciple. I thank you Lord for forgiving me for my sins and allowing me to come as I am. I am willing and ready to give my life to you and for you to use me for your purpose and for your will to be done in my life. In Jesus Name Amen.

(Romans 10:8-13)

Congratulations! You are now a part of God's family, and you are part of the Kingdom. Now get you a bible and start to read it, meditate on it, and understand it. Also start praying daily. Turn from your bad habits and bad works and make good habits and do good works. You will see God move in your life and you will start to transform into someone new. God will bless you and you will also be a blessing to others.

To receive a FREE Holy Bible email me at jdavis4974@gmail.com including this request along with your complete name and address and a small bible will be mailed out to you. This will help you on your journey to learn who the Lord is and the great life you will discover by studying the Word of God, also known as the HOLY BIBLE.

ABOUT THE AUTHOR

To some people I may be this ordinary woman, but not to God! He chose me to speak to His people so that you will be saved and not burn in hell for eternity.

I will never forget the night I had a dream to write but did not know what to write about. All I know is when I woke up, I had this new desire placed inside of my heart. Finally, six years later I discovered what the calling to write was all about, Jesus.

I stood in my kitchen as if I were talking to my cousin about Jesus-how good He is and all the wonderful things about Him and that was my AHA moment!

When I was born, I was a premature baby, weighing 3 pounds and 7 ounces as I mentioned earlier and my parents always told me that I was able to fit in the palm of their hand! Wow, it brings this song to my heart, He got the whole world in His hands! I am thinking something so small is so big-just like God wants all people to be saved and we are so small to Him in size but big to Him in heart. Just like He chose me, to do something so big for Him. To be a voice to all so it can lead people to salvation to have everlasting life!

Let me tell you a little bit about me. The life that I was living really did not have any direction because I did not have a steady relationship with God. I made decisions based off my emotions and my thoughts and what I thought what was right and never asked God what He wanted for my life because I did not know God and honestly, I didn't even know that I was supposed to even ask!

I knew of God but did not know Him personally. I made so many mistakes and bad choices from relationships to indulging in things that were not good for me. At times I used foul language like it was ok as if it were part of the vocabulary. I remember there were times that I approached situations aggressively which eventually led into an argument or a disagreement of some sort.

I was also a very nice and kind person most of the times but honestly, I needed to change into a consistent person instead of being a lukewarm person. People or my loved ones didn't know this battle I was having, they probably just thought I was this sweet person but didn't know how broken I was inside, and this is not who God called me to be!

I lived for me and for the world, but I did not know how wrong I was living and the damage that it was causing internally. Even when I was sinning, I still thought I was such a good person.

To be honest with you, a person can feel like they are such a good person but that won't get you into heaven! Especially when you are intentionally sinning and not even considering how God feels!

I'm so grateful for God's grace and mercy and how the good Lord continued to forgive me through my sins! People may think a small sin is harmless, but it matters because a sin is a sin, big or small!

I remember the day I ran to God because my marriage was not going how I wanted it to go. I was desperate for God and just could not keep going on day to day without Him.

I remember one Sunday I was at church, and I just kept crying because I felt empty without any direction in my life, and I did not know how to make my life better. I just wanted to be and feel free! All along I was already free because of Jesus but I held my own self captive and I was in bondage because I did not have a clue.

I had no wisdom or knowledge of freedom and what belonged to me! In the bible it says, my people are destroyed for lack of knowledge (Hosea 4: 6-7). I did not want to live this empty life anymore because without Jesus, that is exactly what it was.

I was lost! I was born into sin just like everyone else was and I am not proud of the sins that I have done but today I am a different woman, all because of Jesus, not because of me.

I could not have changed without my Heavenly Father's guidance! It was a cry for help! I needed more in my life and the piece that I was missing was Him, Jesus Christ my personal Lord and Savior. This puzzle of broken pieces could not have been fixed without Him and with Jesus, I am whole! He put me together through Him!

I represent the Lord with pride, with courage and boldness! I strive to be better and hope to really be the way God wants me to be while I am living on this earth. His spirit lives inside of me and produces this kind of fruit that should not be taken lightly but lived by and this includes, love, joy, peace, patience, kindness, goodness, faithfulness, gentleness, and self-control (Galatians 5:22-23).

The person I am today cares about how God feels first and then how I feel. I have a conscious and I care about the choices that I make, the words that I speak, and I care very much how I live. It matters because God matters now in my life! All Glory to God because He changed me, and He has never left my side and He is still with me every day! His encouraging words in the bible helped me to be a better person and He taught me how to have control.

When things do not go right, I pray now and seek Him, not just take things in my own hands but if I accidentally take control I must repent because it is always God's way and not my way. God helps me through this journey called life. I had to turn my life to Him because I had problems that only He could solve and if it was not fixed right then and there, He sustained me and held me over by me praying and that gave me peace. I would cry out to Him and that gave me release and eventually the situation was at a cease!

Only God can make things right for you when you focus on Him no matter what the problem is. When you trust God and you give your burdens to Him, He will get you through. He sees your beginning and end, your problems solved right when they begin.

THE END

Made in the USA
Las Vegas, NV
07 November 2021